The poems in *Quilt Life* focus deeply on desire—how women are taught by their families, their church, their intimate relationships that to desire is to risk being denied, or worse, to deserve lashing. The poems lay bare all the sacrifices women make to nurture and accommodate those they love and what happens when what we were taught would fulfill us is gone. Cindy Bosley's fine poems are also a condemnation of the cultural systems that fail to support women in any useful way. Yet, in the face of all life's brokenness, the poems insist on healing, on recovering, on seeking love, on making something downright beautiful out of all the shards. And they insist on desire, always desire.

—Leah Nielsen, associate professor of
Creative Writing at Westfield State University

HARMONY SERIES

BOTTOM DOG PRESS

QUILT LIFE
POEMS

CINDY BOSLEY

HARMONY SERIES
BOTTOM DOG PRESS
HURON, OHIO 44839

Copyright © 2020 by Bottom Dog Press
All rights reserved.
This book, or parts thereof, may not be reproduced in any form without permission from the publisher; exceptions are made for brief excerpts used in published reviews.
ISBN: 978-1-947504-21-9
Bottom Dog Press, Inc.
PO Box 425, Huron, OH 44839
Lsmithdog@aol.com
http://smithdocs.net

CREDITS:
General Editor: Larry Smith
Cover & Layout Design: Susanna Sharp-Schwacke
Cover Image: "Churn Dash Charms" quilt top by Cindy Bosley
Photography: Shannon Smith, Isabel Bosley-Smith,
and Molly Bosley-Smith

Table of Contents

Children's Delight and Hens and Chicks

Gruel	11
Redacted	12
Invisible Studio	15
Invisible Studio at the Farm	16
Spider Jazz	18
Patience of God	19
Reading Neruda, Fighting the Flu	20
Drydock Nightmares	21
The Solemn People Living There	23
In the River	24
Mermaid's Cautionary	25
Guardian	26
Church League at Trilby Field	27
The Morphine Patch	29
'76	30
Poem About the Quiet Farm	31

Baskets and Beggars

Father-Daughter Dance at the Reception	35
Tantric Peach	36
Good Year	37
Fuse No. 12	38
Caged Tigers	40
School Yard	42
After Ten Years, A Confession	44
Invisible Studio with Horse	46
Postcard from the Garden	47
Sunday Morning We Learn of A Friend's Death	48
Funeral	50
Until All the Terrible Things Have Happened	51
Autumn Spider	52
Cancelled	54

CHURN DASH AND SHOO FLY

Pumpkin Season 59
Five Years to Recover from a Marriage 61
Taking Morning Tea 63
Sublet, Rent Control, Apartment Hunting Dream 64
The Logic of Pecans 66
Eavesdropping On *Krishna and Radha in a Pavilion* During the Drought 67
Until Now, I Didn't Know That a Dandelion's Fluffy Ball is Called *Capitulum*,
 and is Made of *Calyx Tissue* and *Cypsela* 70
Precipice 72
On Love and Work 74
A Dollar 76
Envying Rats 78
Because I Don't Know What to Say to Ben Bernanke 79
Dredging the Pond 81
Can't Find My Purse 82
Alzheimer's, Early Onset 83
Fireflies at Pokagon Park 85
Narrative Movements of the Love Object 86
Children of Divorce 87
My Ex-Husband's Husband 89
Ancient Greek Tableau 90
Churn Dash Meditation 91
When I Leave Him, This Will Be Why 93
Lovers by the Water, and also Puerto Rico in 2018 94
Walking in on Lovers During Lent 96
Mystics 97
Sunk Cost Fallacy 100

Acknowledgments 103
About the Author 105

For Laura Whitmore, my sister and friend in every hour.

Special gratitude to Trin, Crown Jewel among friends.

Most sincere thanks to my writing group and to my fellow Kirkmont Kwilters for years of laughter, love, and care.

CHILDREN'S DELIGHT AND HENS AND CHICKS

GRUEL

The middle of the night is like this:
the dry scraping of a stick across a wooden fish,
weasels hanging on the outside screens.
Look at the weapons I have—a newspaper,
some old jars and cotton swabs, a butter paddle:
nothing to stop the wilderness coming toward me.
The house crawls. Its lungs collapse.
An owl and a cat scream at each other in the woods.
Night is simple, like a shovel.

Cindy Bosley

Redacted

It's a fascination
with miniature worlds,
small rooms on chipboard
you can hold in your hand,
built from beads, glue,
and tiny findings,
places only your mind can live.

It's like those hypothetical people
standing in space
atop a platform
hanging in nothingness:
an image employed
in corporate conference rooms
to promote both fear and teamwork.
Those people
might all slip off the edge
if they fail to find balance
in a Simon-Says universe.

It's like in the movie, *Sliding Doors*,
where Gwyneth Paltrow
has three hairstyles and two lives.
One is lived after she catches the train,
and the other when she rides
next to the chatty man
sitting next to the rude man
ridiculous with ear buds and bad singing.
Paltrow loses an earring.

Or it's like the episode
of *Star Trek*—the one
with the time-space shift-hiccup
and all the people on board
step into a slightly off-kilter
version of the present, but can't
even name the un-rightness.

Quilt Life

The glitch rights itself
eventually. But the people
remember an odd, half-instant
deja vu, and each tries to shake it off,
half-smile, something quirky
in the brain, and then
everything continues as it should,
except the peculiarity
trails like the slack rope of a sled
being dragged home
after the hill has gone icy
and the feet are numb.

It's like my friend's farmyard
winters ago, the January lambs' tails
clipped and bleeding on the snow.
Her husband emerged from the barn
in his Carhartt while we
were midwifing bread in the kitchen.
A towel hid the rising on the stove,
and gingham curtains
crossed our faces
as we took healthy swigs of Dos Equis,
our dehydrated limes on the table.

It's those ships in a bottle, sticks
bound with string, constructed
outside the bottle, the tiny parts
threaded together
in ways we can only imagine,
a fishline in the Universe
woven through us all, the silk
and dowel-wadded mess
is berthed through the bottleneck.
Then the magic happens:
an invisible *whoosh*
as the micro-filament is pulled taut
by a large hand, hairy and manicured,

a soul dreaming of ships and oceans.
So the ship appears now, boom
and gaff, canvas sails unfurled,
all hinges set and formed,
a vessel balloons in the bottle,
now corked.

And then, the leap:
how it's like this, yes,
but also like tampons
and IUD's, and both
like the ship, reverse berthed
into the cavity
where they expand
and serve their functions,
and a similar filamented thread
remains. Except…
there was a pregnancy,
and the beautiful ship
did not inflate.

A man I knew
loved the word *redacted*.
Our offices were adjacent,
mine now empty. He
was fastidious and sparkle-eyed.
I like to daydream, still,
that it unsettles him,
as a gentle parasite under the skin,
that he passes my empty office
and does not quite see
the remnants of dust
in the dark room, nor
the circumference of the circle
where my coffee cup was.

Invisible Studio

The ceiling of glass is open
to the sky. The contiguous walls
feature paintings and other arts.

The center of the room is a sandbox
with a bamboo rake and rocks to toss
and kick and think on. Fans circulate

the air and serve as pets. The girl
sits all day in the sun or under a downpour
or inside her snow globe when it's falling

white outside. There is a touch-panel
on one wall where she changes the music,
in and out of categories such as Emptiness,

Smooth Stones, Courage, Ribaldry.
Warmth from the fire is an illusion
and so is the fire itself, broadcast

in holography along a corner tilt.
The chimney is actual brick. The hearth
extends around the room and pillows

circulate. At night, she takes a bedroll
and curls up near Bosch and Bruegel
and wakes as she likes, some days

looking straight into the face of a wolf.
She puts her mittens on and gets to work.

Invisible Studio at the Farm

Every morning, she takes the 10:18 to the farm, and opens
the door, an old wood door with a large flat window,
vintage knobs, and the cherries on the kitchen curtains
wave a little with welcome which she counts on. They
are not the red and white cherries of her mother's kitchen,

but a rebellion of yellow, the deep cherry-green leaves sprout
all around like whiskers on the new kittens in the barn.
She'll visit them when chores are done. First, she takes
the water from the faucet and alchemizes the coffee grounds.
This pours into her one cup with the blue flower, and sugar

softens a harsh, brown river which rises just a bit too much
after so much rain out back. She adds a dash of cream. This
is a one-room farmhouse with four picture windows
and a set of French doors flanking each view like delicate
bouncers in her favorite dream. She puts her chairs

in the middle, and on days when there are four of her, she
sits back to back enjoying every view. Her cat, so fat with
birthings, to watch her nudge under the bed is a visual
mammogram. No one for miles and miles. Purple things
remind her of spring and will launch soon from the ground

like snapdragons, and from the weeds and forests will come
the ivy. She takes a cloth and brushes a little dust around.
She washes a dish. The faucet loosens itself for the cat, a drip
drip drip she takes for granted. Out back, the barn is light
with hay and kittens, pale and more pale, and some stripes

and spots, and some crying—a little kitten crying for her fat
feeding mama so she comes inside. She brings them all inside.
They are happy and peeing in a box, and the table is set as only
she prefers it: one table, a ream of lined paper, sharp corners
and dark lines, and a selection of #2 pencils retiring

for the moment on old Scrabble letter frames someone
nailed to the walls in identical rows, at least twenty. Pencil,
pencil, pencil, and a typewriter, the only modern thing
in the room besides the svelte cat with her tiny moccasins.
Her head is blessed with a paw. She christens her babies

in the sink and the noises they make bring just enough light
to see by, enough to fill the buckets by the door.

Spider Jazz

Spiders don't like jazz.
They don't like sliding around,
the high notes, the blue notes.
Spiders don't like unpredictability;
they like a solid web, the sure thing,
a black purple fly full of blood.

Spiders like opera.

Spiders get nervous with jazz,
jazz gets their hearts beating fast,
their rhythm irregular;
it gets their hackles up.

Jazz makes them uneasy,
they can't do laundry to it,
they can't do their math.
Spiders need strings, bass, a silk-singing long
horsehair breath,
a regular tinkle of piano,
some viola for the soul.

The soul of the spider is tender
and wide. The soul of the spider
spreads like wings,
and you can walk through it,
and you can feel it across your face
in the darkness,
and you know when you've been kissed
by the fishline soul of a spider,
and it startles you,
and that's how the spider feels
about jazz.

PATIENCE OF GOD

At St. Patrick's Catholic Church in Ottumwa, Iowa,
I fell in love with Father Paul at Sunday mass when I was nine.
I married him on my first communion.
At Dickey's Prairie Home Buffet, still wearing my white dress,
I broke a plate and dropped cranberry sauce in my lap
and practiced saying "consummated."

Sitting always in the first pew, I had the best view of him,
and the best piece of the body of Christ, first in line.
Unlike the older ladies whose small tongues quivered,
I had a strong one, and could extend it like a drawbridge,
taking the whole body of Christ on my tongue, securely.
That way, I also stole a taste of the fingers of Father Paul.

Father Paul loved me, I'm sure of it,
which is why he left the church that year.
That's also why my old neighbor next door died.
She loved him too. Father Paul used to visit her
so he could watch me, secretly, as I panned for gold
in the limestone driveway.

Ten years, he said, he'd be back for me, so I practiced
with anyone who'd have me. Father Paul said to—
"Prepare yourself for the coming of the Lord. Make yourself worthy."
By nineteen, I was worthy.
That was a year of heat, a dry year, a year of faith.

Reading Neruda, Fighting the Flu

Pablo Neruda, I forgive you
for falling asleep
with your hand across my face
in the middle of a caress.
You're a good mother.
Some bourbon and honey, a tissue, a lullaby,
a fresh bed.
The rasp in my throat is my own fat love,
choking me.

Pablo Neruda, I'm feverish. My head, a piñata.
The government, even the astronauts
are stumbling on the moon.
And you're not here, tonight. I've done
the dishes, the floor, cleaned
the cabinets, and the draperies.

I am up to no good.
A prairie wind came in,
and blew out the pilot lights
in my stove and the furnace.
I did nothing to save them. Pablo,
I'm learning.

Happiness shrieks through the floor register.
I throw towels
over it, blankets,
pillows, my whole body.
Pablo,
there are no home remedies for this.

Drydock Nightmares

Careful as the jar of yesterday's coffee
in the fridge, the alabaster walls stiffened
and grew cold as I dissolved in sleep.

I leapt free, aloft as snowfall wisping
from the night's cool hand and the city's
sulfur cast of yellow clouds.

Hard rubber tires squealed a stranger's
anger and the naked table with a plate.
A pumpkin on a child's porch grins wicked

and black with rot, one eye hallowed.
My care for you wanders like a homeless lady
in purple, never far away. She is never

far away and seeks my face, everything
and nothing I need. Sometimes a car screech
slithers through the windows

like all I've been afraid of, a plant
across the wall in shadow and other
terrifying monsters when my childhood

room was a playground for demons,
the soil's deep black granules, skin
across farmland, bodies pocking

the prairie, nightmares in every face.
I hope for the best upon waking,
and begin the soup of the lagoons,

duck lice and make-shift beaches,
and the bridges under which no one
goes. Down near the loading dock

CINDY BOSLEY

at the edge of river and stone, a lone
figure inches near the wide doors
of the coliseum, the giant dumpster

of dolls, broken, half alive. My whole life
an empty auction warehouse, my whole
life a basement I'm making my way down.

THE SOLEMN PEOPLE LIVING THERE

In the last room on the fourth floor of the high school,
at the highest point in town,
I felt like an angel,
one of God's slow children, and I could see

my father sitting like a seamstress
in the John Deere plant, threading bolts
with an unfamiliar patience of his hands,
and muttering, "Donna, Donna," in his slow pace.

Past Church Street, past the river, was the roof of my house.
I could see the house exhale, and inside,
the wild dryer, hysterical and vibrating
against the wall like an evil spirit. The windows hissing.

I could see my mother's swollen face,
her big hands on the table, her poor brown clothes.
From the highest point, I could see the thick ice
on the river, and think what it would be to be in it.

Cindy Bosley

In the River

I've been thinking
about the Ohio River.
About the mussels
on the floor of the river,
getting swept under the dock
because I couldn't step on any;
how ugly it was under there.

I've been thinking
about the hands
in the river, about giving.
I've been thinking about you, too,
and my part in this,
your taking
my head in your hands,
your moving me
like a heavy mason jar to your face.

I've been thinking about the river,
the dirty things in the river,
your classroom, about giving.

I've been thinking
of my graduation,
no one coming to see it,
the star on my sleeve,
my coat in my hands
and no one to hold it.
I was thinking about prison,
how even there,
there's someone to take your clothes.

I've been thinking about pride
and that long, ugly river.

Mermaid's Cautionary

Of mermaids, I am one with pink feathering
in my fins, and my hair of wet weed stinks of green
and old water, and also, I live in the cold ponds
where my many sisters also lived. These large lakes,

Great Slave Lake, and the minor oceans, were mine
and my cousins' homes, vacationed by stingray
and the orphaned octopodes, yet warmly attended
by beach fires. Some nights, the tinder and kindling

burned moonlight where we, as betrothed, awaited
our men of sea. Once, though, an equinox rose,
and in the restless, unladylike lust of leisure,
all of us ripened at once. Our nipples, dark

as leeches, our eyes, sharp and chary as the visage
of owls, we were betrayed by our bosoms'
own hunger-swell. Wayward sailors drifted
near enough to toss their thousand copper pennies

toward the shoreline where we plucked them
dreamy-fast. This was how so many were lost.
Distracted by the sparkle of bobbing, turbulent
coins ripped and pushed by tides toward us,

we got caught in their flash and turn, and we
didn't see the shipmen deboard. They were
waiting there, as the water's strong tide eased,
and the coins found homes under rock and weed,

and netting webbed our hair, and the clear water
at our captured feet went stagnant and frothy.

Guardian

I'd like to be one of those
milkweed pods, ripe and popping
open on the fence where little kids
are playing in their sand inside the belly
of a big tractor tire laid on its side.
I'd like to be cotton, little fibers caught
in the girls' hair, I'd like to be shaken free.

I'd like to be the skinned knee of one
of those girls, tended to and favored
just a little by the fingers of the girl,
I'd like to be the knee that was in the air
a bit before falling off the swing.
I'd like to be the swing holding the girls,
a green swing and slide, the cool, slick slide.

I'd like to be the dog of one of those girls, my cold
nose in their palms, my paws on their bellies.
I'd like someone to feed me and play with me
in the water, a kids' pool would be perfect
for a dog like me, dog who loves wet. I could be
the stick they throw, a stick in the hands of those girls
would be neat. Those girls would love me.

If I could, I'd be the tree, the tree of the beautiful girls'
yard, they could tie a rope around me, leave
special toys in my pockets, a firm tree. An eager tree.
If I could, I'd be their mother. I would like to be
their bones, that close. The strength inside them
would be me, holding their arms forward,
pushing back the evil just now entering the yard.

Church League at Trilby Field

I played real softball once, and I made a hit—
not a run, just a hit—
since for once, I was at bat, and had been pulled
from the dugout, as warmed up
as I could get, on deck,
and the ball came at me, which I hate,
but I tapped that ball successfully
with my bat, and I had also bought
a hat for the occasion, and it felt
like childhood to hit that ball,

and in that moment, I revised
every year of gym class
going through school in Ottumwa, Iowa,
back before losing had documented
psychological repercussions, before
those of us picked last were instead
chosen to lead the teams
in the spirit of trying to boost
our inevitable loss of self-esteem,

and in that instant when bat cracked
across ball, and the wad
of chubby softball went piddling
down the middle—*toward*, but not *to*—
the pitcher, which is the most
advantageous way
to accidentally bunt,

I imagined that I was
the hometown scholarship-winning
softball cool-jock ponytail arching
out of hat-back, just right, last name
heat-pressed across the athletic
shoulders of my red jersey,

Cindy Bosley

that fat stitched ball in my one
adult game was moving,
and I was moving,
as in running, and then the ball
was nearly on me, and how
do they DO that, and the baseman
in my grown-up softball game
was about to clobber me
with ball in mitt, and I forgot,
again, deliciously, about my uncool
non-jock history; I went aloft,

as you're supposed to do: give up
everything, sail the air, surrender
body and soul, be the bird,
out-rocket that ball,
and like that, I went flying
on the gravel clouds.

The Morphine Patch

The kids are humming Grandma's tune,
unaware that night is over.
Uncle Rob's gone out to walk the ditch.

We're all thinking how un-right
the attempting sun is:
good weather for rain.

I've been up all night,
settled in the kitchen with the women.
I hear Aunt Edith in the dining room,

dust rag in her hand,
the swish of her grief on the mantle.
The dishes need done.

I throw in cups of stale bread
for a good turkey dinner.
The bread absorbs the broth.

Who would believe it's the start
of summer? It hurts to hold
my heart's idiot hand.

Cindy Bosley

'76

In '76, I wore a halter-top in bicentennial colors,
dainty stars and stripes on my 9-year-old chest.
My brother was born that year like a powerful
winter storm. We lived in our refurbished house

all those years. My grade school had been torn down
and in its place, a McDonald's, so we put on boots
and puddled our way to the new school. Built
in a clover shape, the three pods were named Delphi,

Olympus, and Camelot: strange and foreign ideas
for a tired town. Open classrooms allowed us views
of schoolmates on all sides, no one hiding, no one
unaccounted for. We sat in circles, watched our friends

paint and read in the other rooms. Our parents
thought *chaos*, but it was the 70's, and social life
carried them on its hip like a toddler. Many days,
they did not see us at all, children sifting nails

and sawdust on the living room floor. Small rooms
adjoined other small rooms in quiet resignation
while Merv Griffin held court through dinner,
and Susan Anton flashed my father.

We ate the hard flatness of the table. At night,
my sister and I played *sharks in the water*, jumping
from bed to bed in our make-believe terror
in the room we still shared. We had no puppies

or pets, just our enemies—each other—to hustle out
the cold nights while our friends slept in rotting
comforters down the street, and all our parents
played poker and Twister and guzzled rum,
leaving Uncle Ron to prowl the back bedrooms.

Poem About the Quiet Farm

The land has just been shaved of corn,
the dryer runs all night, the birds are quiet.
Dust from the field makes the outside dirty.
Yesterday, I found the cat's bowl by the barn.
The cat's bowl, (it was empty) and the sheep's bed,
(it was empty) and the grain bin fat with corn.

My husband says the windbreak is a good thing:
a grove of trees you can enter by the gate and be swallowed.
I don't know about that. There's something about swift air
that can hollow out a rotten heart.
Heart like a bad tooth. Wind like a drill. The sky spits.

If I hung the feeder from the barn,
if the birds would come, it might make the winter softer.
It might blow a feline spirit back,
or the early division of a child's soul.

I sometimes see a silver robin, an ancient towhee.
When I don't know the kind, I make it up.
Early on, I inherited my mother's life;
I gave up a child. I would have
named her Little Bird, *peecha, peecha*.

BASKETS AND BEGGARS

Father-Daughter Dance at the Reception

The bride's father hadn't come.
Still, her mother-in-law requested
"Daddy's Little Girl" at her wedding.

The song played. Her drunk mother-in-law
cried while the dad-and-girl pair, the groom's
father, the groom's sister, rocked awkwardly.

The little girl's shy love-eyes ducked into his
lapels, and the father's suit bucked his shoulders
with paunchy air and pucker. The bride

blanched, and stared at her own slippered feet
while the groom grinned, oblivious. The first
rule of dance is that you must protect

your partner. A fall's the worst,
though she's tried not to blame him,
and holds her vows. And yet, the dance.

Her new husband hadn't stopped it. Old
life gone to salvage, new life beyond reach,
blankly she stood, both orphan and widow.

Tantric Peach

Abstinence has sealed us inside
like peaches scalded white
in the gesso of early frost.

Below, in our hotel,
blighted laughter blisters
the tense and crackling voices
of our two nude torsos,
their confused hands touching
the private sleeves of loneliness.

This heart is a Jesuit
to whom I owe a meal.

A strange, lusty grief
heats these parched, blanched,
and pale bones
which aging alone
dries and burns.

Or, softer than that,
but no less raw. In the hall,
laughter so like a girl's,
breaking over rocks like water.

Spying, we witness a sweet
peached husband's wrist
drawing open the door
next to ours.

It's a groom and his bride
after hours, who, ceremony over,
priest gone home, bravely
and with hope enter their room.

Good Year

Inside the tire, trust the rim,
and the rim is what there is to build upon.
I feel increasingly simple
and confident in having little else to offer.

The rim is what there is to build upon,
galvanized metal, chrome, and Teflon.
Confident in having little else to offer,
the tire fills itself with air: a lung with tread.

Galvanized metal, chrome, and Teflon
support the tire and secure the bead.
The tire fills itself with air: a lung with tread
to dress the wheel—the wheel's attire.

Support the tire and secure the bead
for the smoothest automotive ride.
To dress the wheel—the wheel's attire—
is to love your car, to love your car.

For the smoothest automotive ride—
I feel increasingly simple—
love your car. To love your car,
inside the tire, trust the rim.

Fuse No. 12

I'm not the first woman to hate her husband's car.
I even dare to ask him, "How many rides do we take
before you are done talking about all the things wrong

with this car?" The thing is, he's not *critical* of her
imperfections: his is a sweet, pure hope, an even certainty
that he can make her into all she once was, and more.

Not first on his list is switching out fuse number 12—
the cruise control—but it's the least expensive
of the options: air conditioning, brakes, the piece

of interior roofing fabric that requires a 15 dollar
can of spray adhesive. Good as new. Dr. Gary Chapman,
author of *The 5 Love Languages*, would say it's a divine gift

that brought them together: they share the same
love language: acts of service. It's so obvious,
the low humor of it...she needs servicing

and he knows which knobs to twist. The thing is,
she automatically gets all the others: quality time,
words of affirmation, receiving gifts, and physical touch.

The love-book hints that translation is in order,
so my project converts the love metric
into normal measures I can feel. For an hour, I try it:

my hair is sleek enamel, no knots, invites hands,
and then I find my breasts, pointing eastward,
are firmer than I knew they could be, and bright,

and classically-shaped. The strength and support
in my elbows and knees are white-walled, all-season,
ultra-high performance, and it's a bit daunting at first,

but my hubcaps are new as earrings, silver, attention-
getting, but with a certain Walmart modesty, and it's
working, I'm actually feeling *loved*—and I go to tell him

I've figured it out, the key to our long and happy marriage,
there all the time, but then I step through the door onto
the porch, and I see them together: she's jacked up, our

picnic blanket spread, and he's underneath her on his back,
his hands aren't visible but gesture *something* up inside
and the sun is just right, and she might be moaning.

Caged Tigers

There are days
when my breasts, these fat admirals
with epaulets from an opposing army
rebel, blow cover, refuse to hide themselves.

Like children on Christmas,
there are days they wake too early, speak
too loudly from under the blanket, under the bra,
under the blouse. As if they were cats headed for the dark.

Sack filled with rocks,
they resist being bound.
Some days they speak in pain
and sincere distress, as if I've kept them

hidden on purpose,
though it's for their own good:
running slaves living under the floorboards,
Jewish girls behind the false partition. There are days

they insist on being
seen; as if they've been reading
magazines in the doctor's office for over
an hour, they get snippy with the receptionist,

they let the nurse know
just what they think about waiting.
My breasts are fat, lipsticked ladies from
the opera: year after year they sing each other

their most famous arias, tell
bawdy tales about their leading men,
and wear tarnished, glorious gowns (even on non-
theater days), smoke piped cigarettes and drink water

with ice and lemon,
splash of vodka. They've never
been anything like inanimate fruits, never
were content to be the weighty melon, pomegranate,

taut lime: no, with lives
of their own, my breasts wander
the shops, umbrellas tucked tastefully away
for the later rain, no sense of "enough" and no limit

to their spending.
They're bitter, tired of their lives
as working girls, eight and more years
of being pimped out to babies, sore from eczema,

teeth, milk, need.
These breasts want to be wanted.
Want to be admired. Need to be dancing.
Traveling. Seeing the world. Or rather, much more

importantly, having the world
see *them*.

School Yard

After class, the Japanese boys
—my students—and I walk out
to the gated hill beyond which
Tokyo spreads like a frost.

They smoke underage cigarettes
while heavy sky presses the sound
of bicycles whirring past, and I
stand too close to one of them.

The humid air is a skin our words
don't cross. They all talk their own
language, language within language,
speaking Japanese to each other
while I recognize none of it.

The blossoms of their mouths
build a storm. After a few minutes
they bow earnest goodbyes
and go as a group to the buses
which take them to the train,

and some of them ride two hours from here,
quietly shunting past shanties in the dark,
and villages, and bigger towns
like petticoats beyond the city
where gardens around the houses
and walls around the gardens
mark the wealthy, private homes.

Stepping beyond the portico, I turn,
and my umbrella balloons like a soufflé
as it starts to rain. Walking to my apartment,
more than a mile in the rain
toward my weary husband
and sleeping child, the brick path
takes me down through drooping,
spidered, fingering trees,
through part of the city carved
out of this steaming, tropical place
like a tattoo.

Closer now, ferned leaves
whip me home. My skirt, my face,
my eyes are wet, and my legs have had
their completely deserved lashing.

After Ten Years, A Confession

The gangly tropical trees
and the overhanging eaves,
and the centipedes and burgeoning
peonies, the spiral flowers
and spiders. Who could have guessed,
without photos as evidence,
that I was there, my inattention,
my attendance, my youth.

An airplane pummeled me
over the ocean toward this
tropical city. That first morning,
sunlight arrived neither cruel nor pleasing,
but like a sister coming up the walk,
her mood uncertain and convex.

What happened
tangled up the house with vines
like arms. The muted ivy
said nothing, the quiet lampshade
lilies whispered to themselves,
but the tickled rising flowers
grew to wrap the house
in secrecy.

I've never forgotten
leaving a husband at the airport
working out the money to get home,
leaving the child unattended: I was
a whore.

Looking today at those
photographs, I find
I have absolved those involved:
for the first time, myself,
but also the dutiful, angry husband
who returned with me,
and the other one, the one who followed
me back, the storms and squalls
of the heart leading him,
I forgive him too, the patient one
who waited though I did not come.

Cindy Bosley

Invisible Studio with Horse

Inside the studio before she writes,
backed against the wood of a stable stall,
she looks through the window meant
for a horse, some rope, a bit and nails
and the most delicious pudding cake
in place of hay in the trough.

Her rider has sharp spurs
and velvet chaps. The only chair
is a ladder-back, paint crackling,
twine frayed, and holds an armful
of old books at its base.
The inkwell at the windowsill

splashes when the rhythms get right,
her head against the lower wall.
Paper threatens to flutter but the rock
holds them down. Several thrift store
paint-by-numbers of horses, a coyote,
a crow chock the pine planks

around the small, safe room. Her
rider has covered his face in black cloth
and his neck is bare and his chin rises
toward the seasons which are changing
overhead: props for the action. He keens
with low fire. She breathes the sound

and it burns. Horses from the next stall
hear, and they are bucking and showing
teeth and begging them to stop. He doesn't
stop because there's no particular door
to leave through, and because she holds
the letter opener, and the quill,

and the inkwell is never empty.

Postcard from the Garden

In a postcard a friend once sent from London,
his hand, in love with its own penmanship,
scrawled *forevers* and *lovey* and *my bed without you*
and the words wheedled their way under
my eyelids like stops holding open a door.

The door opened. Inside that glossy, billowing bed
dreamed right into the room from a magazine
was a world beyond our own, and we couldn't hold it.
The bed existed in a farmhouse somewhere in Iowa
so far past, we only thought we might have lain upon it.

And we thought about the kisses like pinecones.
And we thought about bodies, drowsy as felines in the barn.
I like taking rubbings of ancient gravestones,
he wrote in the postcard, *there are no nam*es
or dates remaining, and yet, like your mouth,

I know they were once here. In the miraculous bed,
he took my photo; I was kneeling upon a pillow
in the Asian style of lovemaking. *Beauty
of the golden hair* he said, *Breasts
and orange flavored skin,* and it would be a lie

to say he didn't weep. When his notes came,
unbidden as they were but welcome, too, like apples
that don't require touching to be coaxed off the tree,
they flamed open, driving to please me, the reader,
his lover, the one who left him in the garden alone.

Sunday Morning, We Learn of a Friend's Death

Sadness enters the eyes' anterior
chambers as stars, collapsars, and grief.

Each sixty second minute
becomes its own heavenly stylus
into a spiral groove, into a black hole.

"Black hole" is the scientific name
for black hole.

When we walk that spiral groove,
our arms will be outstretched—
gravity, and centripetal,
and centrifugal forces demand it.

We simply accept, eyes closed,
that the asteroids and space debris,
and the occasional on-target rocket
do leave blast holes through space.

"Blast holes" is the scientific name
for blast holes.

When we get there, when we
arrive at the womb-wet warmth
of the soul's tidal pool, the misleading
vista of shells and sand and foam,

we'll feel the soft grit of it, how it coats
the feet first, how it feels not the least bit
acidic, not at all salty, corrosive, or abundant
with foreign bacteria, fungi,
or any of the other strange
fermentations of grief.

The seaside elements will *burn*.

The treacherous devouring of death
never feels the least bit like healing
or salve, or soothing.

The spirit's first, new morning teacup,
porcelain, floral, gilt-edged, and just a touch
under scalding, will not feel drinkable

though it is.

Funeral

Noise of chairs, sputter of the grill—
Midnight, the beautiful lab, is barking.
Midnight's sadness is gone and the trees and trees,
the garble of trees, and the prayers in the trees
sputter in the open-versed poems of honeysuckles.
Not a swab of honey for me, but I give the trees names,
and I can't feel nor will I ever feel the orphaned breeze.
Above the hovering wings, a fluttering forces the air
to move…the fluttering of a soul, the tree-flutter…
and we have never been more quiet, more surprised
by the small noise the chairs make when the bodies move.
The sputter of air becomes speech after we find
what to say, and what we don't say we also leave
out of our prayers. We garble our words and avoid requests,
though our emptiness is like the suburban lawn,
and our grief is separate for each. Our chairs, our trees,
our dying happens separately, but our small deaths
are spent together, envying the air for moving.

Until All the Terrible Things Have Happened

Life is a crew-cut bully
hanging out leisurely
behind a tree,
butterfly knife open,
twirling it like a baton
between his fingers,
t-shirt sleeves rolled up
around a 1950s
cellophane of cigarettes.
He knows you're coming.

After a few really awful things
have happened, you don't
want to know
what else might be ahead.

And after grieving
another recent heart-
rending tragedy,
when you still count
all your children alive
beside you, still feel
your beloved rustling
a sleepy turn in the bed,
still twist on the faucet
for the cat, you just want
to hunker down, cancel
the day's appointments,
get low, greet your knees
in the bright daylight,
scooch under the end
table beside the sofa,
and quiver there.

Autumn Spider

I think about *back then*.
I think I wasn't as *open*,
humbled, longing, lonely...as now.

Like the Tunnel Spider's egg sac,
an act of love I've watched
for weeks now, so *industrial*,
its pod scaffolded between two
glass windows in my dining room,
I think an inner awareness
has pulsed and then burst.

Here in October, toward the end
of the full gestation, the spider
pushes herself against the growing
orb for the sake of the sac's warmth
and the babies planted there.

Soon they will burgeon through
and find their mother's body
surrendered by her, very near,
for their feasting, and I can see
in the window trap,
how she has levered herself
between silk and glass and death
to shield the sac from birds
and the coming cold.

I, divorced woman, am alert,
buoyant, finding my next
frequency even as my human
carriage feels pressed against idea
and memory, as if two panes hold me
protected, something new being born,
and as the cool air freezes,
the leaves falling, the coffee cooling,
a first spider, still unseen, works
through the funnel of the nest,
finds food, lives for food,
and is driven into a future season.

The mother and I
were intimates then. Imagine
our intimacy now.

Cancelled

I was supposed to fly to Missouri today, laughing, rolling
in sheets and sweat with a man I loved for a few weeks,
and also, ashamed, I have to say, we were to be meeting
with a pastor who might have married us, had we lasted

until October. How premature. It is the last days of February,
a leap year, and another 76-year old friend will turn 19 on Saturday.
How time does its funny things. How the heart suddenly
shuts off one day, innocently refusing to feel what it has felt,

repulsed by its own syncopated beats. I knew it could happen
to me, and I, like many, had my abruptly truncated childhood's
lessons: we three children sleeping, father packing up,
father gone before the morning cereal box met the table where

the bowls were not yet dished up. Mother with her cigarettes
on the pre-dawn porch. I knew this kind of day before today,
day where the heart flipflops like a fish on the floor of a room
where the hundred-gallon tank burst its seams with no one

there to hear it nor save the shocking fish, her substantial,
salt-water tank body convulsing on the hardwood in gasping,
arrhythmic slaps, and what must be—how can we watch it
and ignore this—some pain. Today, instead of love and sex

and reunion, is the unexpected, a surprising and comfortable
snow day, my thirteen-year-old child in her bed, still asleep,
while I fry the scrambled eggs and make toast with butter
and strawberry jam, no window-seat, no airplane. Tea

is the way I mark the hours in these raw, oxygenated days,
the heart starving, stretching of dry gills, coughing on the rough
poison of dehydrated air, learning again to breathe. Grief lies quiet,
or so I imagine, under the usual midwestern face, the DNA

of farmers, German and Dutch, stoic in a way that makes us
trustworthy and kind, but also cold, unbending, and winter-driven.
I wonder, though, how much my daughter sees, or senses
in my quiet, desperate, blood-borne longing. Like her, I watched

my own mother stand sentry by our large picture window
overlooking the weathered houses on a blue-collar street,
my father's car a wistful, fading image, my mother's breath held,
face unblanched, while she waited for a date who wouldn't show.

Churn Dash and Shoo Fly

Pumpkin Season

"…they longed to press themselves against a heartbeat." from *The Golden Compass*,
—Philip Pullman

One flesh
doesn't tear
so easily apart.

It's not as clean nor swift
as a severing.

There is no
scalpel-sharp reaving
or silver guillotine.

A marriage ending
does not break
clean apart
but is a bulb-ripe squash
heaved upon the street.

Cleaving
severs, and a gourd-head stem
snaps clean away,
but divorce
is a hollowing,
a scraping of spoon
against the ridged roof
of vegetable—flesh which
the knife ignores.

Rip the flesh out
with the hands.
When the blossom end
opens, you see that teeth
could do a cleaner job.

Cindy Bosley

Stringy flesh quivers
in the lift of lid,
and lingering capillaries
of adoration
no longer pull blood.

Except the brain still says
they should draw blood,
there should be
more life yet.

Some autumn colors resist,
such oranges and greens
are these, the progeny,
and some fruited
veins simply will
never fade: those
of the fire-red leaf.

Five Years to Recover from a Marriage

The books and gurus are discrepant
regarding the time it takes to get one's
life back on a new track that feels real

after divorce. Conventional wisdom
says Get Over It. Those who know better
say that it takes at least three years,

like some locusts, to emerge somewhat
marginally healed and at the helm
of one's new life. Some say it takes

at least one year for every three
of the duration of the marriage.
That means I'm only halfway through.

Some say a year for every five
of the marriage. Some say it never happens,
that divorce is worse than death because

the creature you mourn, the marriage,
includes a being you cannot fully mourn,
your ex-husband, because he's still walking

around, showing up at the bank, unhelpfully
helping raise the last remaining children.
The man you knew is dead, but he is also

still living on your former street. Plus,
he is gay, and there is the new territory
that both of you have boyfriends. I think

that adds a few years. I think that's
a different kind of locust in hibernation,
in stasis, in transformative cocoon.

Cindy Bosley

Life is an experiment. I am the locust
in the cocoon inside a jar inside a glass
aquarium inside a lab inside a politically corrupt

and untenable city inside a firestorm
which does not value the incubation period
of the locust in chrysalis. But my dreams,

when they are not of war, are of yellow hummingbirds
and the most radiant green leaves fluttering
under the daffodils, and the pale butterflies,

blue, and the trees in old age with their beards
of locust casings hanging from each limb,
and a single broken-open locust

dries her wings by drawing upwards, becoming,
in the sun, her own cathedral spanning wide,
grand, opalized, and glorious.

Taking Morning Tea

The teapot itself makes me long for rainy
lovers' mornings near a window. The visible
breath of trees hovers 'round the neighbors
leaving with coffee in their minivans, for work.

Like a fishhook in hope's eczematic skin,
I am tethered to that life. Shame never halted
my lurching heart. I left my husband as if
birthing a cold morning, dark and predictable

like the weather over the lake. Desire escorted
me into a boat. *What might have worked*
drowned in a drink of tea and *ten years later*
was a soft breath to cool the tongue between sips.

Sublet, Rent Control, Apartment Hunting Dream

A building with a view
over a wide river, so beautiful
my own gasp woke me.

Rooms revealed themselves, bigger
than I thought I'd chosen, room
after room, corridor birthing
interior after interior, the number
of sofas nearly choking.

I thought the water would be
magical, and my child and I found
a way out to it, but the magic
had darkness and evil intent:
the oil-thick water rose above us;
the mean eyes and hairless,
dank body of a riverbed creature
leviathaned out of
the necromancing waters.

Back inside, room to room,
lazy as an echo, quick-sand dreams
of escape, running in fields of tar,
latching the doors' locks, so many
more doors to secure, the windows,
unbolted, to hasp, and an eternal maze
of sofas around every wall
and lined in long audience rows.

There was the sudden, bewildering,
over-population of indigent men
who'd been welcomed regularly
by the tenant before me,
the rumors, and the corners
and hands: how to get them out.

Across the floors, as if in a new dream,
chunks of cotton, dried, colored wads
from nail polish remover, and then
the gum wrappers, and then hundreds
of unacceptable teenage letters
crushed into balls. The panned shot,
my view of water, a laceration.

The Logic of Pecans

Like a pinkie finger sliced by the glass
you were washing for your mother-in-law:
the sharp scent of black licorice. Also, the oven's

apple pie. Your wounded finger angles up,
driving home from the urgent care,
as if you were sipping tea with nice people.

You keep your bleeding digit above
your heart. How fascinating, that it
takes so long for the pulse to slow.

The thing is, thinking of black licorice,
there's nothing like it, and only
a few favor anise over other candies.

Cinnamon mixed with refined sugar
sprinkled across deep layers of melting
butter glaciers atop fresh white toast.

Anise chips stand alone in their porcelain
dish. The elderly lady next door, lady
of the wild floral dresses, periwinkle

rosary beads in hand, swore by the healing
properties of pecans, and told me, age seven,
that long ago, before pecans were a delicacy,

apples were the privileged treat, while pecans,
if your grocer's accounts were open to you,
were your only choice for sweet: pie after pie.

Eavesdropping On *Krishna and Radha in a Pavilion* During the Drought

Her eyes close, reclined.
Her face assumes
the expression *impassive*,
and the soul moves
to locate itself—imperceptible—
in her spleen.

Midwestern weather
siphons the life
from acres of plants and grasses,
and the air-conditioners run
all day, all night.

Eyes are drawn
to the labial curves
in the wood of the tree,
even as one hollow seems
to swell into folds, its rounded
mons stripped of bark.

Lying back, tendons
in her hands, tendons
in her throat,
and the thin veils which flex
across her ribs, and the secretive
joins along the neck of her knee,
both knees, and also
those in the ankle relax.
And strain;
relax, and strain.

Drought is a certainty.
Tomato plants grow shy
and old, sheltered in the arms
of the grapevine
along a neighbor's fence.

Cindy Bosley

Pestilence swirls upon the land.
Leaves of a thousand crops
wither, age, and die.

She absorbs the sensuality
of the trees, the large, husky maple
waves its leaves as hands,
and his limbs,
circuitous and leafy,
stroke the air
closest to the ground,
and make buttery the lemongrass.

He is within her as if he is
her bones. He has lain her
breast-down upon the bed,
and—muzzle across
her neck—his rhythms rhyme,
his voiceless, glottal
plosives, gasps of consonants
introduce themselves
in lines of text across her skin.

His hips slap, strap, take—
but then their bodies
whisper again through the refined,
finished pages of translation.

How to describe
the wide open fall
of tree trunks,
having had too little water,
too much sun? Bright
hot fire devours too much;
the midwestern wind
blows dry.

Nature waits, forcing off
conception, and then she waits
for the balding trees to fall,
and then she escorts the water
further out from where
it was before; her stream
wants more than one fish
to swim it,
more than one stone
to line it, more than one
tributary to carry it.
She seeks paths
for new rivulets,
urges them to find a secret,
sinewy, strange, and more fertile
way home.

Cindy Bosley

I Didn't Know Until Now That the Dandelion's Fluffy Ball is Called *Capitulum* and is Made of *Calyx Tissue* and *Cypsela*

We get together every few weeks,
as it happens, some occasion
for one of the children
or the youngest one sick
and in need of hugs
from all who love her.

I come into the house
which used to be mine. Or
he comes up the back
balcony stairs and through
the sliding glass into the one
bedroom, which is hers,
and she's feverishly chilled.

There's him and me,
and I prefer it when his
betrothed is present, too:
the dynamics are less fuzzy,
like a dandelion that's been
blown and discarded: no one
picks it for wishing any more.

At the big dinner table,
someone's birthday, I breathe
in ease to find my seat
left open far from his.
I already know there'll be
food going home cold.

If good luck abounds,
I'll be able to wake
and go to work
and resemble a functioning
person: sit at my desk,
operate the computer,
fetch my tea.

Not like some mornings
after our group meals,
mornings when I remember
there's a light to turn on
with a switch of my fingers,
and I trip on a shoe
and I move to the coffee pot
not registering the ringing
alarm clock, and I pour
my bath, not fully alert
to landlord's tap gone cold,
water heater fritzed again.

I pick up a figurative pencil
and make a mental note
to send an email later today
to have the water fixed.
I file my imaginary note
in an abstract pocket
of a purse I may find next week.

It's Monday morning, so
yesterday's daughter-
centered leftovers are boxed
in the fridge. My coffee walks
with me sloppily in hand,
too much sugar, too little
cream, butter because I have
been taking it with butter.

But then it rests, forgotten
on the edge of the porcelain
tub, and I lay my full body
in the water and find it
also cold, but I lack the signals
to move, so I lie there,
dandelion without cypsela.

Precipice

There is my daydream trip
to the Grand Canyon by rail,

but I don't want to hike the switchbacks down,
nor be carried on a donkey, nor cascade

below the view line in a helicopter of risk.
I just want to look over and down.

I'll have to get close enough,
and I envision this happening on my belly,

doing the iguana crawl
with knees and elbows,

invisible suction in my fingers, my eyes
like summer moons, like the kitten's eyes

when she comes to the edge of the top bunk,
enough sense of potential doom to stay clear

of the lip.
This is me

stepping down the icy metal stairs
in January, snow coming down,

it's dark, hovering zero. Inside, I've just made
and eaten a zesty tuna salad on squares

of baked bread, each flavored bite, such *bite*,
punctuated with cilantro, cayenne, and salt,

diced onion and celery, and peppercorn ranch
to bind, and the fine circles of the last

of the scallions, the last can of tuna,
forked and light, and the bread, warm,

yeasty, hard-crust bread, last of the flour,
last of the yeast, the buoyant loaf

cut with the clean knife, serrated
edge now laid to the side, and the warm

bundle wrapped again in the apron,
clean from the drawer.

This is January,
and the break

between pay grows long. The kitchen
is lean, but there will be more money.

At the top of the stairs in the bad
weather night, my car reading empty,

no heat but gloves and the heartless wind,
a child to fetch from a friend's, no one

awaiting us at home, I must do this.
My parka hood yanked on, forward

of my eyes:
I go down.

Cindy Bosley

On Love and Work

At work, they make me *do* things,
and I get pouty and recalcitrant
and begin spreadsheet plans
to unionize the data entry crew,
all of us grimy with grease
and dirt from overtime
and double-overtime
which we don't *actually* do
because we aren't even hired in yet—
we're just the contractors on lease,
pimped out by the online company
to any that will pay, and we, instead,
count our weekly electronic debits
by the dollar and the ten
with office pens and post-it notes
where the rest of our dreams, in lists,
get made, those fantasies of full hire,
benefits—and we say *bennies*
like the employed ones do,
but they're all headed to HR this week
to chat about their bennies
and their six months to retirement,
while I and the data entry crew
poke fingers at our keyboards,
doing the things they make us do,
sitting in our cubes at our computers,
taking breaks for bathroom,
tea, and chocolates. When things
are really bad, they make us
stuff envelopes, five sheets,
pre-folded, pre-collated, and a card,
and a return envelope, and it doesn't
take a degree to do this, my supervisor
pointed out today, but it helps,
I think, so the mind doesn't
go flat like the left rear tire
on my old Honda, and instead,

I dream of the man who might be
my new boyfriend, and I have
so very much wanted one
for a long time now, because
they say that when you have
love *and* work, that's
true happiness in this life.

A Dollar

When I pay rent this week
my bank account will be overdrawn
by one dollar.

I think about this while I bathe,
five years after divorce, washing
in my strange, educated poverty,

the specialized master's degree
working a ten-dollar job
with no insurance and no 401,

and which cannot, then,
be building interior retirement magic
like straw spun into gold in the sacred

and locked dungeon of my future.
I have less than nothing
by one single dollar.

A day from now, I will have 101
dollars less than nothing
when the bank takes its fee

and the landlord takes his fee
for the inconvenience
my poverty has caused them,

so I will work another day and a half
to fill that gap, and next month,
I will necessarily miss my rent.

Out on a stroll, I meet a cicada
paused on the sidewalk,
dead in mid-flight or dropped

from a bird's beak, or fallen,
blown down, diseased,
from the oak tree's limb, opalescent

and lacy-winged.
Its beauty costs me nothing
but just appears along my path

on a day when I will open a can of soup
I stole from my ex-husband's pantry,
like a succubus having sought

a willing body, or like mites in the ear
of a cat, or like fungus on a diabetic foot,
or like my bank account, drained

into the bleak future
by a compounding deficit owing
to a single dollar I didn't have.

Envying Rats

I think rats have the right idea.
Wherever they go, they keep warm.
Rats nestle under anything,
under each other, under rags or food so old
they don't want to eat it.
Rats smell good things
and go to them, and find themselves
in a heap of stinking trash,
and not smell that at all;
all their meals are enjoyable.
All their nights are warm.
Rats float down sewers together, being rats,
lifting and swimming and sleeping in shifts,
smelling out the good food,
the warmest hole to spend the winter,
the coziest hovel, the best scenery,
the most private place to take their sweeties
and give them a safe piece of bread, a beloved kiss.

Because I Don't Know What to Say to Ben Bernanke

Should you reject yourself because you count buttons and pick up
glass when all civilization tells you: please, this is hardly the time?
—Richard Hugo

I've been sewing bits of fabric
to other bits of fabric and sorting

the plate hangers from the crayons
and then putting them all into the same

large box for some future joy, some day
when I am searching for that one little

red pencil sharpener in the basement
I'll open that box and find my plate hangers!

Find my baggie of crayons! Find
my handbag! I've been carrying toys

long separated from their mates
up the stairs to their owners' rooms.

I've been saving up prompts on notecards
and I don't ever have to use them,

I just need to know they're there. I've been
separating sugar cubes: the ones that got wet

from the ones that are dry. I've been breaking
down boxes and sliding them

with satisfaction into the blue recycle bin.
I've been trading the full recycle bin

on the porch with the empty one outside
by the steps: pleasing and blue and quite empty.

Cindy Bosley

I've been measuring the overdrafts. Calculating
at the CoinStar. I've been moving

the plants around. I've been
very carefully pinning Post-it Notes

to fabric segments and penciling
numbers on each one with flathead

daisy pins which are best for my kind
of work. I've been fixing iced lime-aid

by the glassful: chunk of ice, piddle
of water, slosh of lime juice, and two packets

of yellow sweetener, taking great care
to throw away the empty papers. I've been

stirring my drink with a long iced tea
spoon, slop of a swizzle of vodka,

and making a glass of the same
for others, is what I say.

Dredging the Pond

Mostly at this
now place,
I want to sit in the garden
And wait for winter.

It's time for dating to end.

When I have cleaned
an apartment to move
out of it,
it's so much better.

I want to wind up married.

This summer, I was down
to three eggs
in the gray carton
and then my windshield cracked.

There's so much ugliness.

When what you have
is what I need,
there is no
fair exchange.

Let need rise and be buffeted.

My friend asked why
a woman
would sleep with
someone who repulses her.

That is the whole frog tale.

Cindy Bosley

Can't Find My Purse

"The flesh yearns to converse with other flesh,"
—Stephen Dobyns

And yet, newly dating
in my early fifties, the flesh
has grown weary
from dodging the smokers—

pot and cigarette—
and ducking the abusers,
and swiping left
on the aging sons still living

with their elderly
mothers, and scrolling past
the financially unsound,
and boring through

the born-agains,
evangelical and cruel.
Dobyns isn't wrong,
and yet, here I am,

in dialogue with no one,
absent-mindedly
searching for my desire
like a handbag

I half-remember stashing
on a lower shelf, but which
looked just right
with the burgundy dress.

Alzheimer's, Early Onset

Yesterday, picking up an orphaned t-shirt from my daughter's
friend's house, I drove back and forth down the street, five times,
and back again one more time to see if it was just springtime
and tree blossoms shunting the frost behind them, their insistent
explosion of green keeping the house from looking like its winter self.

The house would not jump out for me. When I called the mother,
busy like me, I had the wrong street. One street over. And it was funny,
but always, the question: when does the forgetting come fully upon me?
There is the note on my office computer, "Class starts at 12:55. Leave
here at 12:47. But only if it's Tuesday. Or Thursday. Note to self."

I have always been absent-minded. Something to laugh at in mid-life.
In class, talking talking talking, and then the word-blank comes like digital
buffering. I ask them, "Oh shoot. It was right here. What's the word for …
when you hunt for something?" They wait politely. It comes to me
and we laugh: "InVESTigate. That's the word." I feel words leak out

like a slow oil drip from the valves of an engine. So slow, the oil change
will refill the—what's the word?—the reservoir (it's okay, it's not
a word I use every day) before anyone ever notices the leak. This
can go on for years. Last week, at a friend's house, something else:
tissue in my hand after a sneeze, I asked, "Do you have a—throwing-

away-place?" "Trash can" had oozed off the mental countertop,
maybe on my way there. I watch for it. I keep notations inside
my very detailed planner. My private notes look more and more
like Aunt Lowana's in the home: "Wake. Bathe. Meds. Food." I check
them off when they are complete, because later, I will look at those bottles

on the counter and have no memory of the morning routine. Maybe
that's normal. Maybe that's menopause. I ask my doctor about early onset,
about testing. I do the puzzles. My brain stays plenty busy. How can it not?
There's so much to remember. My father died of Alzheimer's.
My doctor brushes me off. Says that in ten years, it won't even be a thing.

Cindy Bosley

The research is coming right along, he swears. Meanwhile, my father
died of Alzheimer's and I can't remember if it's Thursday. I hated him
the most of my siblings, but in the worst of it, but just the worst of it,
before it got really bad, during the weeks he still had a cell phone
in his hand and knew that it was for calling people, it was me he called

in the middle of the night leaving messages, "Cindy? Hello? Are you there?"
He didn't remember about voice mail. He didn't even remember answering
          machines.
Can you imagine forgetting so far back that the person who loves
you the least in this world is the one your muscle-memory arthritic fingers
dial in the middle of the night? Think of the valve leak, oil slowly easing

through a seal… for years, quiet, but now: the moment just before bursting.
Think of the full, hot cup, splashing just one—what is the word?—molecule—
onto the hand. Think about the coffee pot left on all day, overheated
but still whole… until that one final instant before it cracks. Can you also
feel the mind's skyward rocketing, an everyday O-ring about to give way?

Fireflies at Pokagon Park

Dark and stars, not the city
sky, but the lake.

Two people on a path,
the walkway no longer
dusty but damp
from afternoon rain,
and the lake,
hopeless with spilled stars,
and the sky in both places.

Fireflies, anxious, cling
inside a jar
inside the cabin,
lid holes punctured
with an awl.

They'll let them go
before sleep.

Surrendered hiking boots
tumble, intimate,
on the mat outside the door.

Zipping together
the sleeping bags,
unfolded and open
to each other,
the couple lies back,
their murmurs aloft.
Hours of talk:
not the easy kind.

Narrative Movements of the Love Object

Combining traditional action and plot
trajectories of the open-ended story,
swinging up to the *dénouement* with chains
gripped and our legs folded back under us

to propel the forward feet, toes pointed,
sometimes toes curling with the gasp of air,
cascading in a rush of high syllabics: Ohhhhh—
for five beats—and I can't have you yet,

your rings still tied to another, your mind
and belly so much mine, however. We stand
in the mire of a damaged, chambered heart—
one withered blue, all-but-functionally-dead,

one quad pulsing, the other snaking 'round,
its spiral design bucking all the old arcs
and fictional tropes, those unforgiving peaks,
those atrophied, raw, double-ended closures.

CHILDREN OF DIVORCE
for M., E., & I.

My child wrapped in the yellow blanket
sleeps beside me because her room
is not ready and this is my apartment
since I have left her father. The two dogs

sleep on the bed with us and the window
is cracked because the heat pumps hard
and we like a little cool. Her eyes do not even
open but she knows I'm beside her

when she says *Mama would you hold me,*
and I do, one arm under her neck
and the other around her middle. We spoon.
She is seven and her hair is thicker

than potato soup. She strokes my hand,
wanting to know why I am so old
but so soft to feel. We both smile
and she flips toward me. My nose

dives to her nose. My eyes romp
in the merry-go-round that is her face.
My child three and a half hours away
at school, but hot-air-balloon tethered,

still texts me in the night, *Mama, tell me
I am better off without him,* and it is my own
electric question in the hollow hours.
My answer is unwaveringly *yes*, a sure

and solid *yes*, even if my hand shakes
in the morning pouring the coffee. This
daughter calls me again to tell me how she
didn't mean to gain a good thing next,

but like a key starts a car, she has managed
to do so anyway, and my pride in her
blossoms like drops on the windshield
to a downpour. Still, our hearts want

their hopeful reassurance: *tell me I am better
off without him.* My middle child sleeps
in her blue and brown room with her pale
Labrador at her father's house and watches

criminal shows where every dark and bloody
mystery is solved. If she could just stand still,
if the world could just stand still, she could
get used to all the changes, if she would just

be held, if she would consent to being loved,
comforted, confused, if she believed what
none of us dares to quite believe, if she could
just trust us: *It's going to get easier. It won't always

be this hard. We love you as we always have, we
who have betrayed everything you ever knew.*

My Ex-Husband's Husband

It's been too much,
these weekends sharing
meals for someone's new
boyfriend, someone's farewell
dinner, someone's birthday.

"Why can't you just have
a normal divorce?" a guy
I dated said to me once.

Sometimes hatred comes back,
an acid attack, a torrent of hail,
especially on mornings
at my desk when I am bored
and dread the place I work.

Other times we iron
things out, lots of messages
sent, received, responded.

Still, it's a force
hitting hard, chest-
against-steering-wheel
hard, like an autopsy:
the impact tore his heart
from its arterial frame.

Like that, for me,
some Sundays—
when you, man who was
my twenty-two-years'
husband, touch
his hand, the hand
of your husband.

Ancient Greek Tableau

The ultrasound technician goes fishing
with her one-eyed wand, because
for the third time, the IUD has pulled
its strings up inside me like
a plumber retracting his snake.

I am not the crazed Medea nor
the Cyclops raging with an eye.
No day with blood in it is a usual day.

The lab techs take special care,
because even though the full-spectrum tests
are routine for many: employment, care
of children, care of the sick, somehow
like fortune tellers, they know the
tourniquet and jab is not routine for me.

Perhaps it's in my face—not
the Medea face, but the Leda face—
darting, nervous lips, chewing hands
pressed between my knees. So unlike
the earlier posture, prone
in stirrups before the midwife.

My eyes look away while the tubes fill.
The blood already carries
its answers like fortune cookie papers
fresh off the printer, cut and peeled
and folded, already tucked into
edible confection to be broken open.

The news comes like usual:
pale scraps like white feathers
blowing from the greedy
beak of the swan.

Churn Dash Meditation

I.
At home alone in a striped bra, I browse
the internet for poster-size images
of the known universe. You probably
know the ones—those maps of the multiple
galaxies that say: You Are Here.

You've probably watched digitally
animated versions online, their titles
coming up as Facebook memes dressed
like scientific articles which exponentially,
with hypothetical light years,

expand the situation where you are
so that you are illustrated as a cosmic
molecule and can finally feel
your smallness, your own
instantaneousness.

You are a cup-o'-noodles, carrot
and pea and corn kernel, reconstitute-able
in under three minutes. I, fellow human,
am a teabag of herbs and leaves.
We think we know we roam

across earth as if on a piece of barley
fallen loose from the measuring cup
headed to the crock pot. And we are
so literally bits of nothing, empty
like the gap where my key

hangs on the ring. Is it
any wonder, then, that everything
ripples in packets, not waves,
carried by the energy
of fear and loss?

II.
I've been listening to a couple meditation
guys on audiobook. I am here, but only
for a speckle, a pock, a grain of black pepper
in a spice jar among jars in the spices
factory, just one black pepper

fleck in the vat of pepper flecks,
each of us. Mostly what I feel
is the gravity of spin, the force
of living, beings trapped by speed
and a mean face on the merry-go-

round. And I'm searching for
the Milky Way poster because
I think it would help pass the—
blink of an instant—years
thickening like a churn of butter,

a child grinding that handle,
the churn so heavy, the butter
thickening, the dash doesn't want
to move, and we are here, round
stick in a square hole, churning,

or mortar and pestle: simple tools,
in the powerless, fleeting hands—
if the universe has hands—
and I'd have to check that map,
the highway rest stop has one, surely,

but they say human pains pass, hurts
fade. The universe, though, will expand
forever. The unified field is open.
Come on, let's crush each other.
It'll be over in less than a moment.

When I Leave Him, This Will Be Why

I have sometimes wept
in lovemaking,
the overpowering boundarylessness
of it, pleasure bouncing against
pleasure, and nowhere for the eyes
to go but closed.
Sometimes it has been scary
when someone else's desire
won out over the other's decline
in entanglement, but the most
crushing moment
came when I stretched,
awkward with ideas and metaphors
to explain the meaning—
the infinite new horizon,
the universal scale tipped
in our favor, the glorious
body of his body in my body—
and my words caught
in my tears like
gauze and twigs,
and my voice tremolo'd
before it was even audible,
before the breadth of the fully
transformed soul, when,
in the nakedness of raw, bare,
breathless love, he said,
"Damn, girl. That was fun."

Cindy Bosley

Lovers by the Water, and also Puerto Rico in 2018

It's not my way to write a poem
about the thickets by the stream,
two figures walking there, a he
and a she.

And it isn't my style to thread in
the political, like a roll of paper towels
tossed in glee toward a whole group
of people in need.

It just isn't how I do things,
to discuss the imagery of that first
thicket, how sensual and thrilling,
how like birth

when the two lovers emerge, safe
and wise and private, flushed,
and fingering their hair. It doesn't
suit my persona

to name the gloating monster among
the needy, the way his manicure hides
the word *manure*.

Destroyed people have needs. Life
and death. Yet, the lovers still deserve
their garden of wilderness and purity.
They belong

walking the curve of that stream, enjoying
their fantasies of each other, holding hands,
or hand to pinkie, their hiking boots
mash a path

through the woods where they will always
live, his love masquerading in a sweet,
milky trickle down her inner thigh. People
elsewhere die,

ships of supplies at the shores, no one
to distribute, no system, no forces
at work, just a dumb world.
No fair.

Cindy Bosley

Walking in on Lovers During Lent

Scenes of intimacy
in the movies are starting
to feel foreign, a privacy
I intrude upon,
remember making
those sounds.

Now I beg pardon
of the television screen:
my own prudish gasp.

Turning
    —for the sake of their privacy
away
    —from my flushed embarrassment
to my book stack,
I pull down *Living Lent*.

It's the fourth Monday.
Somewhere in a wilderness,
fingering the barks of maples,
I walk with my tap and spile.

Listening for a willing tree,
I find them swollen
with desire and temptation
and resistance.

Love is not what
I meant to give up.

Mystics

1.
There are hundreds of Catholics, disheveled but Sunday-dressed
and sitting with little space between them. Some pockets are empty
in the crowd, pockets of coats and pockets of absence in the pews.
One or two ladies will faint before the end of mass, it is so hot
and it is always the ladies who faint.
They are overcome with Christ, I prefer to think,
and images of their own Interior Castles.

2.
The priest has some sense of his grandness, sashaying
the aisle, one boy with the bible, one boy carrying
the cross. We observe as the priest's pale, bored face
reenacts the theater before us. It's a minor holy day,
so the incense pot is cantilevered across the vast
sanctuary as if it were a head, and we think immediately
of St. John the Baptist, and also King Herod,
but there are 15 verses referring to beheadings
in the Bible. *Unfortunate end,* someone mutters
who is also thinking these thoughts.

3.
Father, it has been seventeen months since I have set foot
in your holy building. I like the singing though.

4.
Some think it easy to visit a church alone. I myself
have often walked to mass. First as a girl because my mother
did not go, but insisted I must, and then
as a divorcee, walking down the steps from my apartment
and over a few yards. Grandmother would be pleased
I lived so close, but disappointed that I spent
so little time there. She knew better than I did
that I'd never be a nun. She told me,
a child who just confessed a kindergarten crush,
that the faint freckle on my ring finger meant a man would never
want to marry me. My first answered prayer
was that the freckle disappeared.

5.
Why did my sister and I do it? Why did we
strike out for Saturday confession before Easter
just because our mother said so? Why did we sit,
one by one, in the dark room with only the priest
and the other shamed person on the other side of the priest
with his or her screen closed but listening quick
for every word, as, of course, we all did?
Why didn't we take off for the grocery store,
which was closer, and bother the market man
and buy some brightly colored jaw breakers
with our alms money? Mother forbade us
to light the votives near the statue,
and we obeyed that too, except for the one
I lit by praying it would light.

6.
To walk into a church alone, now, is to wear
a bright coat of flame. I prefer to sneak in,
completely unseen, to move like Strider in Lord of the Rings,
wearing a black hood and smoking a pipe, sulking in a corner.
I want a mission as grand and dangerous as Frodo's
with a wizard and a dragon where now I have
a coffee cup, and a pen, and a bed in the same room where I cook.

7.
And the ring I want
is one of marriage, still. Who knew
how tricky it would be to find.

8.
I think only once have I ever made love
with a man who loved me in equal measure to my
love for him. I'll never know if I'm right about that.

9.
From kindergarten class, I walked home alone and lost
some papers every day. My mother scolded me and I cried.
At Halloween, it was my number drawn to win the class
pumpkin. When my mother arrived, she talked to me
about sacrifice, talked me into leaving the gourd behind
for another child who might not have a pumpkin.
At St. Patrick's Day show and tell, the rough boy Russell
showed his four-leaf clover, bound delicately
in cellophane, and we were told the clover was magical
but grew commonly. For many Springtimes yet to come,
I hunted my back yard for any common and delicate
squares of cellophane.

Sunk Cost Fallacy

Today is the six-week mark
tallied by my boss who said
could be three weeks,
could be six, until my full-hire
from temp to real, my
fully functional citizenship
with benefits and an HR
department, and a right
to the free immunizations
for flu, required of all bodies
on the payroll or not.

The *sunk cost fallacy*
explains how long
a person will wait for a bus
before walking away,
calling a cab,
dissolving into thin air,
having already invested time.
I'm living the fallacy;
I've been waiting at the corner
for the bus.

Dallas, Texas, 1987,
waiting for the bus
that never came:
the wait seemed sure
and finite. The bus, as busses do,
would definitely come.
After some time passed,
well, maybe not *my* bus…
still, any bus could come.
So I waited four, then six,
then eight feet back from the curb
to be missed
as people threw things
from passing cars: apple core,

pop tab, crushed soda can, snot-
encrusted Kleenex.

How could I know
to call the station, to learn
that the bus had broken down,
the route rerouted that day,
and how could I know
that no matter how many, ten
more minutes, fifteen more
minutes, maybe another ten
more minutes, no bus
was ever going to come?

Standing in ignorance,
my only certainty was that
to leave my spot
would surely mean
missing the bus
which would, of course,
eventually come.

I can, here today,
give notice.
But then, how would I know
that the day after departure,
me, gone with my pens, my corporate
logo stress ball, my cubicle décor
in bags, the job would post at last?

And if it's not about the bus
or my boss, then
I'm the obvious constant
and also the missing element
as the Sunk Cost Fallacy
meets an Old Wives' Tale
meets the Heisenberg
Uncertainty Principle,
and my life unfolds with thinning faith:

Cindy Bosley

as long as I stand here
measuring time, the bus
is never coming,
the watched-for public
transportation vehicle
will never boil,
and I cannot ever be certain
of anything, except that
back in Dallas, I did,
at some point that day,
turn around, take
my few steps back
to the berm, move
my feet along the infinite
stretch of road,
and find my way home.

Acknowledgments

"A Postcard from the Garden" first appeared in *Prairie Schooner*.
"After Ten Years, A Confession" first appeared in *Flyway Literary Journal*.
"Funeral" first appeared in *The North American Review*.
"Gruel" first appeared in *Passages North*.
"In the River" first appeared in *Immediate as Air*.
"Influenza" (appearing here as "Reading Neruda, Fighting the Flu") first
    appeared in *The South Florida Poetry Review*.
"Patience of God" first appeared in *Willow Springs* and then was reprinted in
    Anthology of Magazine Verse and Yearbook of American Poetry.
"Poem About the Quiet Farm" first appeared in *Midwest Quarterly*.
"The Solemn People Living There" first appeared in *Prairie Schooner*.
"Spider Jazz" chosen as first runner-up in the Asher Montandon Award Contest
    sponsored by *Hyper Age*.

About the Author

Cindy Bosley grew up in Ottumwa, Iowa, a *M*A*S*H* town, and is a long-time resident of Toledo, Ohio. Her writing brings together the arty and practical traits of her resilient and generous mother, and the eclectic, philosophical nature of her John Deere factory-floor father. In addition to poetry, Cindy is an essayist, quilter, and miniatures artist. "I love building small worlds on a plate." Cindy has been twice married—once for two years and once for 20 years, and is proud of her three daughters, Emma, Isabel, and Molly. Cindy Bosley currently works in the credentialing corner of the health care field and has taught writing and literature full and part-time much of her adult life. She shares her home with her youngest daughter and their two cats, Maddie and Ella Diablo.

Bosley's local writing group has been meeting for 25 years, and their gatherings provide the deadlines which keep her productive. An alum of the Iowa Writers' Workshop, class of '91, Bosley is the author of the chapbook, *The Siren Sonnets* (Finishing Line Press 2016), and her poems have appeared in many literary journals. She has two essays in a college composition textbook, *The Composition of Everyday Life*, and has shown her miniatures in area shows, and has a quilt published in a quilt book featuring a favorite technique.

"At the heart of things, I'm a tactile person, a fiber artist who plays with fabric and with language in the same way. 'Images as fabric bits' feels most true to how the stories in the poems are made. My poems always start with a feeling. An atmosphere. A momentary picture shows itself, and it's my job to ease it out, trust its possibilities, and see how it attaches to other scraps. I join it to other stray and fraying bits and segments and keep sewing the images together—as far as their moments allow. And then a little bit more after that. A favorite writing teacher's best advice was to avoid taking the first exit out of a poem, and that's been my goal with any art-making."

BOOKS BY BOTTOM DOG PRESS
APPALACHIAN WRITING SERIES

Mama's Song, by P. Shaun Neal, 238 pgs, $18
Fissures and Other Stories, by Timothy Dodd, 152 pgs, $18
Old Brown, by Craig Paulenich, 92 pgs, $16
A Wounded Snake: A Novel, by Joseph G. Anthony, 262 pgs, $18
Brown Bottle: A Novel, by Sheldon Lee Compton, 162 pgs, $18
A Small Room with Trouble on My Mind,
by Michael Henson, 164 pgs, $18
Drone String: Poems, by Sherry Cook Stanforth, 92 pgs, $16
Voices from the Appalachian Coalfields, by Mike and Ruth Yarrow,
Photos by Douglas Yarrow, 152 pgs, $17
Wanted: Good Family, by Joseph G. Anthony, 212 pgs, $18
Sky Under the Roof: Poems, by Hilda Downer, 126 pgs, $16
Green-Silver and Silent: Poems, by Marc Harshman, 90 pgs, $16
The Homegoing: A Novel, by Michael Olin-Hitt, 180 pgs, $18
*She Who Is Like a Mare: Poems of Mary Breckinridge
and the Frontier Nursing Service*, by Karen Kotrba, 96 pgs, $16
Smoke: Poems, by Jeanne Bryner, 96 pgs, $16
Broken Collar: A Novel, by Ron Mitchell, 234 pgs, $18
The Pattern Maker's Daughter: Poems,
by Sandee Gertz Umbach, 90 pgs, $16
The Free Farm: A Novel, by Larry Smith, 306 pgs, $18
Sinners of Sanction County: Stories,
by Charles Dodd White, 160 pgs, $17
Learning How: Stories, Yarns & Tales, by Richard Hague, $18
The Long River Home: A Novel, by Larry Smith,
230 pgs, cloth $22; paper $16
Eclipse: Stories, by Jeanne Bryner, 150 pgs, $16

APPALACHIAN WRITING SERIES ANTHOLOGIES

Unbroken Circle: Stories of Cultural Diversity in the South,
Eds. Julia Watts and Larry Smith, 194 pgs, $18
Appalachia Now: Short Stories of Contemporary Appalachia,
Eds. Charles Dodd White and Larry Smith, 178 pgs, $18
Degrees of Elevation: Short Stories of Contemporary Appalachia,
Eds. Charles Dodd White and Page Seay, 186 pgs, $18

Free Shipping.

Books by Bottom Dog Press
Harmony Series

Quilt Life, by Cindy Bosley, 108 pgs, $16
Family Portrait with Scythe, by James Owens, 114 pgs, $16
The Pears: Poems, by Larry Smith, 66 pgs, $15
Without a Plea, by Jeff Gundy, 96 pgs, $16
Taking a Walk in My Animal Hat, by Charlene Fix, 90 pgs, $16
Earnest Occupations, by Richard Hague, 200 pgs, $18
Pieces: A Composite Novel, by Mary Ann McGuigan, 250 pgs, $18
Crows in the Jukebox: Poems, by Mike James, 106 pgs, $16
Portrait of the Artist as a Bingo Worker: A Memoir,
by Lori Jakiela, 216 pgs, $18
The Thick of Thin: A Memoir, by Larry Smith, 238 pgs, $18
Cold Air Return: A Novel, by Patrick Lawrence O'Keeffe, 390 pgs, $20
Flesh and Stones: A Memoir, by Jan Shoemaker, 176 pgs, $18
Waiting to Begin: A Memoir, by Patricia O'Donnell, 166 pgs, $18
And Waking: Poems, by Kevin Casey, 80 pgs, $16
Both Shoes Off: Poems, by Jeanne Bryner, 112 pgs, $16
Abandoned Homeland: Poems, by Jeff Gundy, 96 pgs, $16
Stolen Child: A Novel, by Suzanne Kelly, 338 pgs, $18
The Canary: A Novel, by Michael Loyd Gray, 196 pgs, $18
On the Flyleaf: Poems, by Herbert Woodward Martin, 106 pgs, $16
The Harmonist at Nightfall: Poems of Indiana, by Shari Wagner, 114 pgs, $16
Painting Bridges: A Novel, by Patricia Averbach, 234 pgs, $18
Ariadne & Other Poems, by Ingrid Swanberg, 120 pgs, $16
The Search for the Reason Why: New and Selected Poems, by Tom Kryss, 192 pgs, $16
Kenneth Patchen: Rebel Poet in America, by Larry Smith,
Revised 2nd Edition, 326 pgs, Cloth $28
Selected Correspondence of Kenneth Patchen,
Edited with introduction by Allen Frost, Paper $18/ Cloth $28
Awash with Roses: Collected Love Poems of Kenneth Patchen,
Eds. Laura Smith and Larry Smith with introduction by Larry Smith, 200 pgs, $16
Breathing the West: Great Basin Poems, by Liane Ellison Norman, 96 pgs, $16
Maggot: A Novel, by Robert Flanagan, 262 pgs, $18
American Poet: A Novel, by Jeff Vande Zande, 200 pgs, $18
The Way-Back Room: Memoir of a Detroit Childhood,
by Mary Minock, 216 pgs, $18

Bottom Dog Press, Inc.

P.O. Box 425 /Huron, Ohio 44839
http://smithdocs.net

www.ingramcontent.com/pod-product-compliance
Lightning Source LLC
Chambersburg PA
CBHW021018090426
42738CB00007B/816